D1713120

NORSE
GODS, HEROES, AND MYTHOLOGY

BY A. W. BUCKEY

CONTENT CONSULTANT
Lilla Kopár, PhD
Associate Professor of English
The Catholic University of America

Core Library

An Imprint of Abdo Publishing
abdobooks.com

Cover image: Odin is one of the main gods of Norse mythology.

abdocorelibrary.com

Published by Abdo Publishing, a division of ABDO, PO Box 398166, Minneapolis, Minnesota 55439. Copyright © 2019 by Abdo Consulting Group, Inc. International copyrights reserved in all countries. No part of this book may be reproduced in any form without written permission from the publisher. Core Library™ is a trademark and logo of Abdo Publishing.

Printed in the United States of America, North Mankato, Minnesota
092018
012019

THIS BOOK CONTAINS
RECYCLED MATERIALS

Cover Photo: North Wind Picture Archives
Interior Photos: North Wind Picture Archives, 1, 12–13; Album/Fine Art Images/Newscom, 4–5, 20, 34, 43; Red Line Editorial, 9; British Library/Science Source, 11; Shutterstock Images, 17; New York Public Library/Science Source, 18, 27; Karl F. Schöfmann/imageBROKER/Newscom, 22–23; akg-images/Newscom, 30–31; Stringer/Reuters/Newscom, 36–37; Walt Disney Studios Motion Pictures/Photofest, 40, 45

Editor: Marie Pearson
Series Designer: Ryan Gale

Library of Congress Control Number: 2018949765

Publisher's Cataloging-in-Publication Data

Names: Buckey, A. W., author.
Title: Norse gods, heroes, and mythology / by A. W. Buckey.
Description: Minneapolis, Minnesota : Abdo Publishing, 2019 | Series: Gods, heroes, and mythology | Includes online resources and index.
Identifiers: ISBN 9781532117855 (lib. bdg.) | ISBN 9781532170713 (ebook)
Subjects: LCSH: Norse mythology--Juvenile literature. | Norse gods--Juvenile literature. | Heroes--Juvenile literature.
Classification: DDC 293.1--dc23

CONTENTS

THE TREASURES OF THE GODS

L oki, the clever trickster god, had just gotten himself out of trouble. He had stolen the beautiful golden hair of the goddess Sif. Luckily, he was able to convince some master craftsmen to make new hair for Sif. These craftsmen were dwarfs. Dwarfs lived in mountains and rocks and made tools and jewelry out of metal. They hammered gold into fine, silky wires. Sif's new hair looked even more beautiful and fit on her head perfectly. But seeing the dwarfs' golden handiwork made Loki greedy. Now Loki wanted more treasures.

Loki frequently causes trouble in stories from Norse mythology.

GOLD IN NORSE MYTHOLOGY

Gold plays a large role in Norse mythology. Norse poets sometimes called gold "Sif's hair" because of the new hair she got from the dwarfs. The gods' most precious jewelry is made out of gold. A god named Heimdall has gold teeth. One famous Norse story tells of a cursed gold ring. The ring drives family members to crave it so badly that they murder one another trying to possess it. The story warns of the dangers of greed.

Loki went to two dwarfs named Brokk and Eitri. Loki bet Brokk his head that Eitri could not make a treasure better than Sif's golden hair. The dwarfs agreed to the bet but said that if they succeeded, they would have Loki's head. Eitri made a boar out of pure gold and a magical golden arm ring. The ring created eight new gold rings every nine days. But he had one more treasure to make.

Eitri forged a hammer that would never break in any battle. The hammer would always hit its target. Best of all, it worked like a boomerang. It came back to the person who threw it. All the gods loved this magical hammer. They gave it to Thor, the strongest god. The dwarfs won the bet and asked for Loki's head.

But Loki wasn't ready to give up so easily. He pointed out that he had bet his head but not his neck. The god dared Brokk to take off his head without taking off even one bit of his neck. Brokk knew that this was impossible. He'd been tricked. He was furious. Brokk decided to sew Loki's mouth shut instead. He wanted to keep him from tricking others. But Loki broke out of the stitches. He has had a crooked mouth ever since.

NORSE MYTHOLOGY

The story of Loki, Brokk, and Eitri is a classic of Norse mythology, the collection of beliefs and stories that are important to Norse culture. The gods of this story are treasure lovers. They need weapons for war. They do not always keep their promises. And even though they have magical powers, they are not immortal—they can get injured or die.

OTHER NORDIC CULTURES

The Norse were not the only traditional culture in and around Scandinavia. The Sami people have also lived in the region for thousands of years. Sami and Norse people traded, but they had different cultures and beliefs. In addition, Finnish myths and cultural traditions are different from Norse and Sami ones.

Norse mythology is a term for the beliefs and stories of Norse culture. Norse culture existed in the northern European countries of Sweden, Norway, Denmark, Iceland, and other nearby areas from approximately the 600s to the 1300s CE.

Their stories, or myths, were part of a traditional religion and way of life. Like all myths, these stories feature supernatural characters and events. They also contain truth. Myths help explain the world. They tell where people come from and where they are going. They also show which gods and values a culture thinks are important.

The Norse people survived in cold, harsh lands. They worked and lived alongside many kinds of animals.

WHERE NORSE PEOPLE
LIVED

The Norse people lived in what are now Sweden, Norway, Denmark, and Iceland. What can you tell from the map about the landscape of these places? How do you think this influenced Norse peoples' daily lives?

ICELAND

SWEDEN

NORWAY

DENMARK

Some of these animals, such as wolves and boars, were dangerous. One of the most famous groups of Norse people were the Vikings. Viking culture lasted from the 800s through the 1000s CE. The Vikings made their living as raiders and settlers. They traveled the sea in ships called longboats. Vikings attacked the coasts of Northern Europe and the British Isles. They took land and valuable goods. Often, they burned the villages they raided.

The gods and goddesses of Norse mythology lived dangerous lives. Norse mythology is full of magical animals, including wolves, ravens, and goats. The gods could be violent and warlike. The gods spent their lives preparing for the most dangerous battle of all. They got ready to fight a battle for the entire universe.

The Vikings were expert sailors.

GODDESSES, GODS, AND GIANTS

Norse mythology tells of a long war between gods and giants. The first being in the universe was a giant named Ymir. Odin, the leader of the gods, came afterward. He is the grandson of Buri, the first human. Odin and his brothers killed Ymir and created the world out of his body. Since then, the gods and giants have been at war. They are relatives as well as enemies, since some of the first giants had children with the first humans. It is said that their fight will end in the final battle of the world.

The goddess Freyja is sometimes shown riding in a chariot pulled by cats.

ODIN'S FAMILY

The gods live in a world called Asgard, near the top of Yggdrasil, the universe tree. The world of humans is called Midgard, or Middle Earth, and lies in the middle of Yggdrasil. It is connected to the world of the gods, Asgard, by a rainbow bridge called Bifrost. Asgard has many halls where the gods dwell. Some humans are also brought to Asgard to be rewarded after their deaths.

Odin, the leader of Asgard, is a god of wisdom, knowledge, and war. He has powers to see the future and is always ready to learn more. Odin has two ravens that report to him what is happening in the world. Their names are Huginn and

TYPES OF GIANTS

Today, *giant* means very large. But not all Norse giants are large people. There are different kinds of giants, such as frost giants and fire giants. Trolls are giants who are very ugly. There are also very beautiful giantesses, or giant women. Sometimes the gods want to kill the giants. Other times they marry giants.

Muninn, which mean "Thought" and "Memory" in Old Norse. Odin only has one eye. He gave the other one away to know more about the future. Odin practices magic and travels far and wide for wisdom. He wants to know what will happen at the end of the world. He knows that is when fate says he will die. Once, Odin hung himself on the giant tree Yggdrasil for nine nights so that he could learn the runes. The runes were an alphabet that could record secrets and work magic.

Odin's wife, Frigg, is a goddess of love and marriage. She also can see into the future. Odin once said that he believed Frigg knew everyone's fate. Unlike Odin, she does not choose to use this power. The only time she tried to change fate was to protect one of her children.

Odin's most famous sons are Thor and Balder. Thor is a strong god, a god of thunder, weather, and fertility. He is warlike and loves to fight giants with his magical hammer. He is married to Sif. Thor has a chariot pulled by a pair of magical goats. The goats also provide him with a food source, as he can eat their meat over and over again. Thor is known for being brave.

Thor's brother Balder was nearly perfect. He was beautiful to look at and very wise and kind. Balder's mother Frigg once made everything in the world promise never to hurt him. But she forgot to ask a young mistletoe to promise. The gods would sometimes throw things at Balder because he would not get hurt. One day, Loki tricked Balder's blind brother Höd. The trickster told Höd to throw mistletoe at Balder. Höd had no idea the plant had the power to kill. Balder died and went to live with Hel, Loki's daughter, in the underworld. Hel is the goddess of the dead. Her body is half-dead, half-alive. Balder could not leave the underworld, and his mother felt great grief. Balder's brother Vali killed Höd in revenge.

YGGDRASIL

Yggdrasil is a tree that holds the universe. The top of
the tree shelters Asgard. The gods use the bridge called
Bifrost to connect to Midgard, the world of humans. Bifrost
is a rainbow. Underneath Yggdrasil is the underworld, where
the souls of the dead go. The well where Odin left his eye
in exchange for knowledge is also in the roots of Yggdrasil.
Why do you think the Norse people saw the world as a tree?

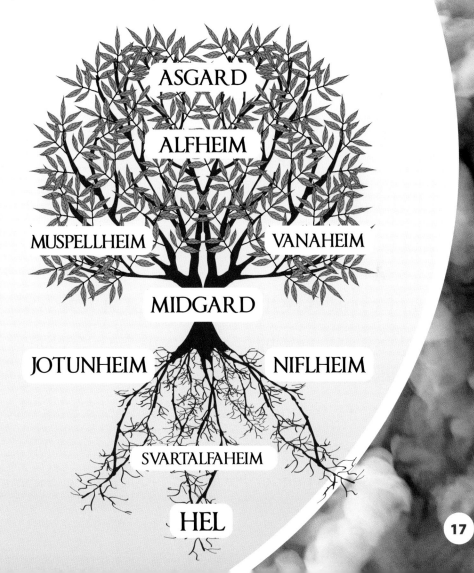

An Icelandic manuscript depicts Höd, *left*, under Loki's influence, *center*, killing Balder.

OTHER GODS AND GODDESSES

Loki is a god of many contradictions. He is the son of a goddess and a giant. Loki lives with the gods in Asgard. Sometimes, though, he seems to be on the giants' side. Loki is known as a trickster god. He can change his shape and his gender. He is good-looking and charming but cannot be trusted. Yet even after Loki helped kill Balder, he and the other gods sometimes go on adventures together.

The god of the sea is named Njord. He has twin children, a son named Freyr and a daughter named Freya. Freyr is a handsome god of fields and crops. His sister Freya is a beautiful goddess of love and fertility. She has a husband who has left on a long journey. She also has many lovers. Freya travels in a chariot pulled by cats.

THE AESIR AND THE VANIR

There are two groups of gods in Norse mythology. Most gods, including Odin, Frigg, Thor, and Balder, are part of the Aesir. The Old Norse word *æsir* means "gods." A smaller group of gods are called the Vanir. Njord, Freyr, and Freya are part of the Vanir. According to Norse myths, the Vanir came from another place and joined the Aesir. Some historians think that the Vanir were originally gods from another culture. They may have been mixed with Norse gods in ancient times.

In one Norse story, Loki steals Freya's necklace. Heimdall, *right*, finds and returns it.

Njord is in an unhappy marriage with Skadi. Skadi is a giant, but she is also the goddess of hunting and skiing. She and Njord can never agree on where to live. She misses the mountains while he always wants to be near the sea.

There are many other gods who live in Asgard. There is golden-toothed Heimdall who guards the bridge Bifrost. He keeps watch over Asgard. Tyr is the one-handed god of justice. Bragi is the god of poetry. The gods also have spouses and many children.

STRAIGHT TO THE
SOURCE

In the Old Norse poem the *Poetic Edda*, Odin recalls the time he hung himself on Yggdrasil to get knowledge of a writing system called the runes:

> I know that I hung
> On the wind-swept tree
> All nine nights
> With spear was I wounded
> And given to Odin,
> Myself to me,
> On that tree which no one knows
> From which roots it grows.
>
> Bread I was not given,
> No drink from the horn,
> Downwards I glared;
> Up I pulled the runes,
> Screaming I took them;
> From there I fell back again.

Source: Snorri Sturluson. *The Prose Edda: Norse Mythology*, trans. Jesse L. Byock. London: Penguin, 2005. Print. 145.

Consider Your Audience

Review this passage closely. Consider how you would adapt it for a different audience, such as your parents or younger friends. Write a blog post conveying this same information for the new audience. How does your new approach differ from the original text, and why?

DWARFS, ELVES, AND MAGICAL BEASTS

G iants, gods, and humans were not the only beings in the Norse universe. The world that Norse people knew was also home to elves and dwarfs. Norse mythology mentions dark elves and light elves, though the difference between the types is not clear. The myths do not give a lot of information about what these elves look like. According to Norse tradition, the light elves live in Alfheim. Alfheim is a heavenly place owned by Freyr.

Norse mythology is full of many kinds of creatures, including an eight-legged horse named Sleipnir.

Norse mythology reveals more about the dwarfs who live inside the mountains and rocks. These dwarfs were created by the gods out of maggots, the small, burrowing wormlike larvae of flies. The dwarfs are skilled blacksmiths and metalworkers. They make tools and jewelry for the gods.

DRAGONS AND SERPENTS IN NORSE MYTHOLOGY

In Norse mythology, dragons are large, evil, and snakelike, with poisonous breath or bodies. Some Norse dragons walk on the ground, but others do not have feet. Fafnir is a famous dragon who guards a golden treasure and has poisonous blood. A legend tells how the heroic young Sigurd kills Fafnir.

THE ANIMALS OF YGGDRASIL

Yggdrasil holds all types of magical animals. An eagle sits atop the tree. A hawk sits on top of the eagle's head, right between its eyes. Four male deer, or stags, live there too and eat the tree leaves. Yggdrasil is home to a squirrel named Ratatosk.

Ratatosk runs up and down the trunk of the tree telling gossip.

Farther down the tree sits Heidrun, the magical goat. Her udders produce mead, an alcoholic drink made from honey. Dead warriors whom Odin picks to go to a hall called Valhalla drink Heidrun's mead. Valhalla is one of the many halls in Asgard. Valhalla is a special hall for human warriors who have died bravely in battle. Odin keeps these warriors so that they will help him one day in the final world-ending battle, Ragnarok. In the meantime, they fight all day and then celebrate by drinking and eating. Besides drinking Heidrun's mead, the warriors at Valhalla feast on the meat of a magical boar named Saehrimnir.

A dragon named Nidhogg gnaws at Yggdrasil's roots, slowly killing the tree. One day, he will come flying as an omen, or sign, of Ragnarok. Another famous snakelike monster is the Midgard Serpent. He is a giant sea snake who wraps himself around the human world.

He keeps his tail tucked in his mouth to form a circle.

He marks the boundaries of the known world to humans

and keeps good and evil in balance. The Midgard

Serpent is one of Loki's sons. According to myth, the Serpent and Thor are destined to kill each other at the battle of Ragnarok.

RAVENS IN NORSE MYTHOLOGY

Ravens are symbols of knowledge and death. Odin always worries that his two ravens Huginn and Muninn will not return after he sends them away each day. He says that he worries more for Muninn. Norse poets called ravens "swans of blood" because they showed up at battles to pick at the bodies.

LOKI'S MAGICAL CHILDREN

Loki has many children that look like creatures. One is an eight-legged horse named Sleipnir.

This is the horse that Odin rides. Loki also has three

children with a giantess. These three children are the

Tyr, *right*, loses his hand when the gods bind the wolf Fenrir with magical chains.

goddess Hel (who rules the underworld), the Midgard Serpent, and Fenrir the wolf. Fenrir the wolf came to live with the gods after he was born. He grew big and strong very quickly, and the gods became afraid of him. They decided they would try to chain him up. Fenrir easily broke through all their chains. Finally, they made a magical chain to put on Fenrir. The wolf was worried he would be tied up forever. Fenrir asked the gods to promise to free him if he could not break the chain himself. The god Tyr promised by putting his right hand in Fenrir's mouth. They put on the magical chain and Fenrir realized he was stuck for good. Angry, Fenrir snapped his jaws and bit off Tyr's hand. Fenrir will fight against the gods in the final battle for the universe.

STRAIGHT TO THE
SOURCE

In this passage, the gods learn that Fenrir the wolf has been born. They watch him grow up. They decide to make a magic chain for his leg that will keep him in one place.

With . . . an ogress who lived in Giant Land, Loki had three children. One was [Fenrir], the second was the Midgard Serpent, and the third was Hel. When the gods discovered that these three siblings were being brought up in Giant Land, they learned through prophecies that misfortune and evil were to be expected through these children . . . [and] harm was on the way, first because of the mother's nature, but even more so because of the father's. . . . The Aesir raised the wolf at home . . . but the gods saw how much the wolf grew every day and knew that all the prophecies foretold that it was destined to harm them.

Source: Snorri Sturluson. *The Prose Edda: Norse Mythology*, trans. Jesse L. Byock. London: Penguin, 2005. Print. 154.

What's the Big Idea?
Read the text carefully. What is the main idea of this passage? Give two or three pieces of evidence to support your answer.

CREATION AND RAGNAROK

I t all began with a giant, some ice, and a cow. The giant was Ymir. He made new giants with his sweat. Then the first cow, Audumla, licked the ice until another creature appeared, a man. He was Buri, grandfather to Odin. Odin and his brothers killed Ymir and most of the giants. They made the world out of Ymir's body. Midgard was created.

RAGNAROK

Norse mythology does not only tell stories about the distant past. It also tells tales about the distant future. The stories predict that the

An artist's depiction shows Yggdrasil with the Midgard Serpent wrapped around Midgard.

world will end in a great battle between the gods and the giants. The battle will be so huge that it will destroy life as it is now. The battle will happen at the end of times, called Ragnarok. The gods know a lot about what will happen when Ragnarok comes. But they do not know when it will arrive.

Before Ragnarok, there will be three winters full of war followed by three very long and harsh winters. A giant wolf, possibly Fenrir, will swallow the sun and moon. The Midgard Serpent will come out of the sea and onto the land. Fenrir and the Midgard

THE WEAPONS OF RAGNAROK

Norse mythology tells of several famous objects that will be used at the battle of Ragnarok. The fire-giants will attack the gods on a ship called Naglfar. The ship is made entirely out of the fingernails and toenails of dead people. Vidar, a son of Odin, will battle and kill Fenrir. During their fight, Vidar will be protected from Fenrir's bite by a pair of thick, magical shoes. Norse legend explains that all the spare bits cut from the soles of human shoes were used to make Vidar's shoes as strong as possible.

Serpent will attack the gods. Loki will come with an army of giants. Odin will come with his chosen warriors from Valhalla.

The myths foretell what will happen at Ragnarok. Most of the gods will die. Odin will be swallowed by Fenrir the wolf. Thor will kill the Midgard Serpent, but the Serpent's poisonous breath will kill him too. Loki and Heimdall will kill each other. Midgard will be destroyed.

Finally, once the battle is over, the sun's daughter will rise in her

SELECTING WARRIORS

Valkyries are supernatural women. They appear on the battlefield to help Odin decide which warriors should die and join him in Valhalla. Odin sometimes purposely selects the bravest and best warriors to die because he wants them to join him. Therefore, human fighters cannot always trust Odin to help them in battle. The Valkyries, too, can be fearsome or they can be protective, as they have the power to choose whom to kill and whom to keep safe from harm. Valkyries also serve food and drink to the warriors inside Valhalla.

Thor, *holding hammer*, fished for the Midgard Serpent before Ragnarok.

mother's place. A few of the gods will survive, including Thor's sons and Odin's son Vali. Balder and Höd will come back from the underworld and be friends and brothers again.

Then, a new world can begin. Crops will grow by themselves and the earth will be green. One man and one woman will survive and eat the dew from the grass. Their children will repopulate the earth.

Knowing that Ragnarok will come one day helps explain why the gods do some of the things they do. Odin searches for wisdom and gathers warriors. He does this in hope that he can save his own life when the time comes. Thor kills giants because he knows they will be his enemies in battle at Ragnarok. Loki shifts his loyalty back and forth. He is a god, yet he knows that in the end, he and his children will fight on the side of the giants at Ragnarok.

EXPLORE ONLINE

Chapter Four talks about Norse myths about the beginning and the end of the world. The website at the link below also gives information about Norse beliefs and stories. It shows pictures of Viking weapons and art. Does the website answer any questions you have about what Norse people believed?

VIKINGS: BELIEFS AND STORIES
abdocorelibrary.com/norse-mythology

THE LEGACY OF NORSE MYTHOLOGY

Starting in the 900s, most people in Norse lands converted to a new religion. This religion was Christianity. The Norse religion began to fade as Christianity took its place. However, Norse stories and traditions did not disappear. People still told old stories and made traditional art. Sometimes Christian crosses even had images of old Norse gods and heroes. One of the most famous sources for Norse mythology is a book by Icelander Snorri Sturluson. He was a Christian who lived

Some people, including those belonging to the Asatru Association, are continuing the worship of Norse gods today.

SNORRI STURLUSON

Snorri Sturluson was an Icelandic politician and author. Many people in Iceland converted to Christianity in the 1000s, so Snorri grew up a Christian. However, he was fascinated by traditional Norse stories. He collected and retold them in a long book, known as the *Prose Edda*. The *Edda* preserves many famous Norse myths and legends. It also contains information about the traditions of Norse poetry.

from 1179 to 1241. He wrote the old stories down.

REVIVAL OF PAGAN NORSE RELIGION

In the 1800s, some people from Scandinavia decided to bring old Norse beliefs back in a form of paganism. They started a religion sometimes called Odinism or Asatru. This religion was based on the belief in Norse gods. Today, several thousand people practice Asatru. Approximately 4,000 of them live in Iceland.

Most people who follow Norse beliefs today are peaceful. However, some people have used images of

Norse gods and goddesses to support racist beliefs. They think of Norse stories as part of a heritage that belongs to white people. And they use Norse symbols to promote the idea that white people should have more power. This is not a practice that the Norse people would have understood. Norse mythology did not support racism.

NORSE MYTHOLOGY AND FANTASY

The Norse myths have been a powerful source of newer stories and myths. In the middle of the 1900s, a British writer named J. R. R. Tolkien wrote

J. R. R. TOLKIEN

J. R. R. Tolkien was a British professor and author. He was born in 1892 and started publishing books in 1937. He taught and did research on medieval English literature and Old Norse myths. Tolkien even invented his own languages to use in his stories. Some of his inventions were inspired by Old Norse words. For example, the name for the setting of his stories, Middle Earth, is borrowed from the Norse Midgard. The dragon Smaug in the book *The Hobbit* is named after the Old Norse word for "crept."

Chris Hemsworth starred as Thor in the Marvel films.

a book called *The Hobbit* and a multivolume novel
called *The Lord of the Rings*. The world of the books
was inspired by Norse mythology. Tolkien named the
dwarves in his story after Norse dwarfs. One of his main
characters, Gandalf, was based on Odin. And the story
of *The Hobbit* and *The Lord of the Rings* is similar to
an old Norse story about a cursed ring. *The Lord of the
Rings* became a movie series. Tolkien's books and their
movie adaptations are some of the most famous fantasy
works of all time. Publishers estimate that *The Lord
of the Rings* books have sold more than 150 million

copies. This Norse-inspired tale changed the fantasy world forever.

Another popular Norse story found its way into comic books and movies. The character Thor in Marvel comics and movies is a strong god who comes from Asgard. Like the Norse Thor, he is always ready for a fight. He is tricked by Loki. And he also has his magical hammer for battle.

Norse mythology has not been forgotten. Like Loki, it can take on many forms and charm many audiences. It is ancient but full of surprises, even today.

FURTHER EVIDENCE

Chapter Five discusses Norse mythology in modern life. What is the main idea of this chapter? What are three pieces of evidence that support this point? Read the article at the website below. Find a quote from the article that supports the chapter's main point.

THE "TRUTH" ABOUT THOR AND LOKI
abdocorelibrary.com/norse-mythology

FAST FACTS

Gods and Goddesses

- Balder is a wise, kind, and beautiful god. He is the son of Odin and Frigg. Loki tricked Balder's brother Höd into killing him.

- Frigg is a goddess of love and marriage. She can see the entire future but does not tell what she knows. She is married to Odin.

- Hel is the goddess of the dead. She is Loki's daughter and lives under Yggdrasil.

- Loki is a trickster god. He is the son of a goddess and a giant. He is charming but cannot be trusted.

- Odin is the leader of the gods. He is wise and loves magic and war.

- Thor is a strong god of thunder, weather, and fertility. He carries a magical hammer.

Creatures

- Fenrir is a giant and powerful wolf. He is the son of Loki and a giantess. He will kill Odin at Ragnarok, but he in turn will be killed by one of Odin's sons.

- The Midgard Serpent is the son of Loki and a giantess. He lives in the sea encircling Midgard. The Serpent and Thor will kill one another in battle at Ragnarok.

- Sleipnir is an eight-legged horse and one of Loki's sons. Odin rides on him.

- Yggdrasil is home to many magical beasts, including an eagle, a hawk, a dragon, four stags, a goat, and a boar. Ratatosk the squirrel carries gossip to the gods.

Stories

- The story of the creation of the world tells how Odin and his brothers killed Ymir and most of the giants in order to make Asgard and Midgard. The gods and the giants have been enemies ever since.

- The story of Ragnarok tells how in the future, gods and giants will fight at the end of times. Most of the gods will die, and the Sun and Earth will be destroyed. After the battle is over, a few gods and two humans will rise and make a new world.

STOP AND
THINK

Say What?

The world of Norse mythology is full of unfamiliar terms. Find five words in the text that are new to you and look them up in the dictionary. Then write the meanings in your own words and use each one in a sentence.

Another View

Chapter One tells the story of how the god Thor got his famous magical hammer. As you know, every source is different. Ask a librarian or another adult to help you find another source for this myth. What is the point of view of each author? How are they similar and why? How are they different and why?

Surprise Me

Chapter Three describes magical animals in the world of Norse mythology. After reading this chapter, what two or three facts about Norse mythological animals did you find most surprising? Write a few sentences about each fact. Why did you find each fact surprising?

Why Do I Care?

Chapter Five describes how the tales of Norse mythology have influenced movies and books in modern times. Have you read or watched books or movies that make reference to Norse mythology? How would the world be different without this mythology?

GLOSSARY

craftsmen
people who have a special skill for making things

culture
beliefs, art, language, and other customs shared by a group

fantasy
a genre of fiction that involves unusual or otherworldly settings and characters

fate
a destined course of events that lead to a result that no one can change

fertility
the ability to produce offspring or crops

pagan
having to do with people who worship many gods; these people may include witches and priests of ancient Celtic religions

racist
having to do with a belief that one race of people is better than another

raider
someone who suddenly and aggressively invades other territories

settler
someone who moves into a new territory and begins living there

supernatural
beings and events that do not follow the laws of nature

ONLINE RESOURCES

To learn more about Norse mythology, visit our free resource websites below.

Visit **abdocorelibrary.com** for free Common Core resources for teachers and students, including vetted activities, multimedia, and booklinks, for deeper subject comprehension.

Visit **abdobooklinks.com** for free additional online weblinks for further learning. These links are routinely monitored and updated to provide the most current information available.

LEARN MORE

Crossley-Holland, Kevin, and Jeffrey Alan Love. *Norse Myths: Tales of Odin, Thor, and Loki.* Somerville, MA: Candlewick Press, 2017.

INDEX

About the Author

A. W. Buckey is a writer and tutor living in Brooklyn, NY.